Think like an Astronaut! How Do Rockets Work?

Science for Kids
Children's Astronomy & Space Books

pfiffikus
EDUCATIONAL BOOKS FOR CHILDREN K-12

To witness the launch
of a space rocket,
even on television,
is very fascinating.

Let's discover
the truths
behind the
rockets that
take man
to space.

A space rocket uses the force from hot gases to move forward.

It does not work by pushing back air because in space, there is no air.

Most of the rocket's fuel gets used up during the launch to arrive at an escape velocity of a minimum of 7 miles a second or about 25,000 miles per hour.

This is the speed that the rocket needs to travel in order to escape Earth's gravity.

How does a rocket engine work?

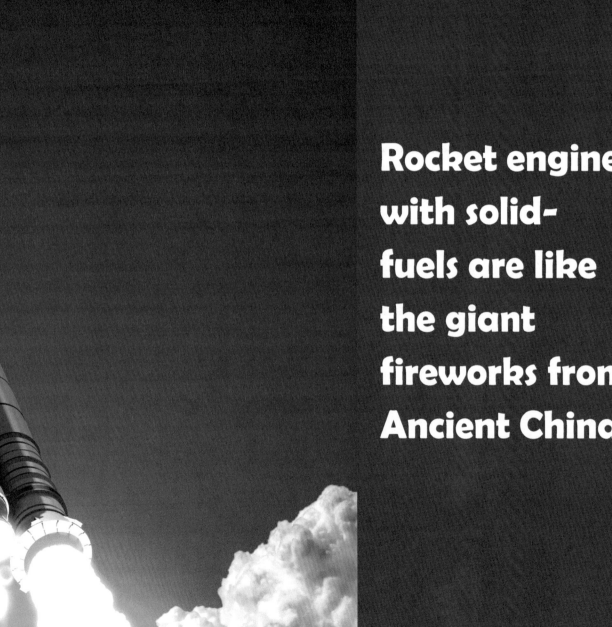

Rocket engines with solid-fuels are like the giant fireworks from Ancient China.

While these rocket engines are powerful, they cannot be controlled or powered off in any other way. That is why these are normally used only during lift off.

Unlike the engine of an airplane jet, which takes air in as it soars in the sky, the engine of a space rocket with solid-fuels has to carry its own supply of oxygen.

Remember that there is no oxygen in space.

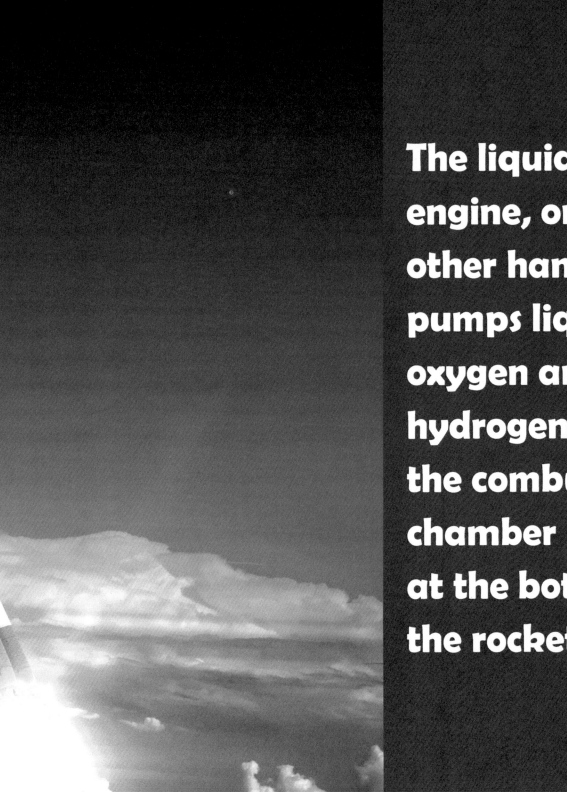

The liquid-fuel engine, on the other hand, pumps liquid oxygen and hydrogen into the combustion chamber placed at the bottom the rocket.

It burns the propellant, and allows hot exhaust to escape through the jet nozzle in order to create a thrust.

Both hydrogen and oxygen are burnt at the highest temperature to make the rocket's engine more powerful and efficient.

However, prior to the combustion process, both hydrogen and oxygen are stored at the lowest temperature in order to keep them in their liquid form.

In addition, low temperature cools down the nozzle and protects it from generating heat at the time of liftoff.

Unlike the solid-fuel engines, switching on and off of liquid-fuel engines during liftoff are controlled by the use of valves.

To travel to outer space is a once-in-a-lifetime adventure, but not all of us can have that chance.

But if you study hard enough and work towards becoming an astronaut, then maybe someday you'll be able to ride a rocket ship and blast off to space!

Made in the USA
San Bernardino, CA
17 December 2017